THE WISDOM OF THE TAOISTS

THE AUTHOR

D. Howard Smith was, from 1953 to 1966, Lecturer in Comparative Religion at the University of Manchester, where his special field was Far Eastern religions, particularly Chinese philosophies and cults. He was for over twenty years a missionary in China and now, in retirement, lectures at Lancaster and Newcastle-upon-Tyne. He is the author of various books including Chinese Religions *and was the Sectional Editor for China and Japan in the* Dictionary of Comparative Religion *edited by Professor S.G.F. Brandon.*

Published by
NEW DIRECTIONS

THE WISDOM
OF THE TAOISTS

COMPILED AND TRANSLATED FROM THE CHINESE BY
D. HOWARD SMITH

A NEW DIRECTIONS BOOK

Manufactured in the United States of America
First published as New Directions Paperbook 509 in 1980 by arrangement with Sheldon Press, London

Library of Congress Cataloging in Publication Data

Main entry under title:

The Wisdom of the Taoists.
(A New Directions Book)
  (Wisdom series)
    1. Mysticism—Taoism—Collected works.
I. Smith, David Howard. II. Series: Wisdom series
(New York)
BL1923.W57   299′.51442   80-15629
ISBN 0-8112-0777-3 (pbk.)

New Directions Books are published for James Laughlin
by New Directions Publishing Corporation
80 Eighth Avenue, New York 10011

TABLE OF CONTENTS

THE WISDOM
OF THE TAOISTS

★

STORIES AND SAYINGS

THE WISDOM OF
THE TAOIST MYSTICS

THE great Taoist mystics flourished in China in the fourth and third centuries B.C. in a period known as the Warring States (401–221 B.C.). It was a time of political and social unrest and of great intellectual ferment. China was divided into a number of independent principalities whose rulers sought for a political philosophy which would ensure peace and prosperity to their people, increased power for themselves and hegemony over the whole land. The rulers, with but little understanding of the arts of government, sought the advice of learned men of various schools of thought – Confucians, Mohists, Legalists, Sophists, Logicians. In return they offered positions of prestige and dignity, and lavished wealth and honours on those whom they trusted. To these blandishments of the rulers the Taoist mystics turned a deaf ear.

Like other learned men the Taoists inherited a traditional wisdom handed down from earlier times, but whereas the Confucians and others were mainly concerned with the establishment of an acceptable political and social system, the Taoists sought individual perfection, a deeper insight into the mysteries of nature, and union with a cosmic principle which they believed to underlie all existence. Unlike the Confucians, who disdained a rich folklore and the beliefs and practices of a shamanistic religion, the Taoists took great delight in tales and legends which emphasized the marvellous and the supernatural. Stories in the books of Chuang-tzŭ and Lieh-tzŭ tell of 'perfected men' *(chih jên)*, 'realised men' *(chên jên)* and 'sages' *(shêng jên)*; men who could perform magical feats, live entirely on air and dew, induce in themselves a trance-like state, roam at will through the universe, and who had attained to such perfection that they could save men from disease, avert calamity and bring prosperity. No doubt these stories were meant to be allegorical but many Taoists regarded them as factual. This gave rise to a belief in 'immortals' *(hsien)*, who, having attained immortality by means of yoga, interior hygiene and alchemy, had entered a heavenly hierarchy, exercising spiritual control over the world under a supreme deity.

Disillusioned by the scheming, intrigues and sycophancy of the feudal courts, and highly critical of the social conventions, elaborate ceremonial, moral precepts, and detailed rules of behaviour which formed a veneer to cover hypocrisy and self-seeking, the early Taoists contrasted the artificialities of man-made institutions with the ordered sequences of natural processes. They were horrified by the enslavement of the peasantry, the wasteful and destructive wars, the endless jockeying for position and power. They believed that man, like all other creatures, must learn to conform to the spontaneous and natural processes of birth, growth, decay and death, and become attuned to a cosmic rhythm. Freedom, peace and happiness for all men could only be attained by conformity to natural and not man-made laws. They accepted the teaching of Yang-chu (fourth century B.C.) that man's most prized possession is life itself. Their aim was to be left alone to enjoy life in freedom, preserving their own inner integrity. Fame, glory, wealth, honour, even to gain the whole world, were as nothing to one's own life. Retreating into the countryside, living frugally with few desires, they spent their days in contemplation of the wonders of nature in all its varied forms. They sought to penetrate to the heart of that ever-changing and evolving process which they saw everywhere around them. They sought to preserve life, their most important possession, as long as possible and even to attain some form of immortality. From hermits and recluses of an earlier time they learned the value of silent meditation, fasting, and yogic practices by means of which they purified the mind and body.

Taoists believed that the whole cosmos is spirit-fraught, and that there is a spiritual dimension to man himself. Yet few saw reason to believe in a creative, purposive God. The whole universe – gods, spirits, men, living creatures, even the inanimate fields, rocks, hills and streams – were all seen as part of an ever-changing process at the heart of which lay some principle of unity, so hidden and mysterious that its secrets could not be penetrated by human reason or intellect. To seek and find that mysterious principle, to discover it within one's own inmost being, to observe its workings in the great universe outside, and to become utterly engulfed in its serenity and quietude came to be the supreme goal of the Taoist mystics. Apprehending it to be ineffable, impalpable and nameless, they nevertheless gave it the name TAO.

The teachings of these Taoist mystics were incorporated into much of the literature produced in their own time. This Taoist literature became an inspiration to future generations, leading to a philosophy of life which acted as a counter-balance to the prosaic and practical emphases of orthodox Confucianism. It proved to be a per-petual fount of inspiration within the cultural and religious life of the Chinese people.

Though the names of several of these Taoist mystics have been preserved practically nothing is known of their personal history. Legends and stories concerning them are scattered through numerous works of this period; *Kuan-tzŭ, Huai-nan-tzŭ, Lü-shih-ch'un-ch'iu* and many others. But the main works on which we depend for an understanding of their teachings are *Chuang-tzŭ* and the deservedly famous *Tao-Tê-Ching*, which is attributed to Lao-tzŭ.

These early Taoist mystics of China differ greatly from the Christian, Jewish and Muslim mystics of Western tradition. These latter were all heirs of a biblical belief in one supreme creator God, conceived of as a personal spirit, holy, wise, all-powerful and good. Their life of contempla-tion, and the spiritual exercises which they per-fected, led to an utter commitment of the soul to God in an ecstasy of love. Their aim was to attain to a beatific vision and the complete union of the soul with its maker. The wisdom of the Taoist mystics is more akin to what we find in the Upanishads of ancient India which taught that Brahman alone is real, the source and sustaining energy of all that is. In a quietude in which mental activity is stilled the Indian *rishis* entered into an ecstatic trance in which all differences were resolved and absorption into Brahman attained. There is little positive evidence to suggest a direct influence from India on early Taoist thought, but there are slight indications that the forest dwellers and the wandering ascetics of India were not entirely unknown to the Chinese in the third century B.C. It was a time also when the Chinese, expanding southwards, were being influenced by the beliefs and ideas of subject peoples. It may well be that Taoist mysticism owes much to alien influences.

Turning to the two main sources for our understanding of Taoist mysticism, *Chuang-tzŭ* and the *Tao-Tê-Ching*, we find that they are anthologies of Taoist sayings, stories and anecdotes, and cannot be ascribed in their present form to the men who, according to Chinese tradition, are supposed to have written them. Their authorship is unknown. Compared with their teachings the name or fame of their reputed authors mattered little. The term Taoism was first used by scholars of the Han Dynasty to indicate a corpus of teaching which ran contrary to the traditional thought and institutions of that time. Their teachings expounded two fundamental concepts: those of the Way (Tao), and its efficacy (Tê).

7

The book of Chuang-tzŭ contains thirty-three chapters, of which the first seven were written by Chuang-tzŭ himself. Many of the subsequent chapters bear the impress of his mystical and poetic genius and his mordant wit. Practically nothing is known of his life. He lived in the fourth century B.C., a native of Mêng in present-day Honan, a small state already incorporated into the powerful state of Sung. Chuang-tzŭ for a short time occupied an unimportant post in the city of Chi-yüan in Mêng, but he soon left it to become free and independent. Attempts were made to persuade him to take high office in the neighbouring state of Ch'u, which he repudiated. He preferred, he said, the freedom of a pig wallowing in the mire to the tinselled trappings of a sacrificial ox being prepared for the slaughter. Though seeking freedom to follow his own inclinations, he was by no means a recluse. He had many friends who recognized his great philosophical and mystical insight. He loved to poke fun at the Confucians and Mohists of his day, and engaged in constant debate, especially with his friend Hui-tzŭ, the logician.

A superficial reading of Chuang-tzŭ might give the impression that he preached a doctrine of irresponsibility and licence. This is quite untrue. By delving deep into the nature of things and into his own nature he sought for a secure basis for the good life. He recognized that there is a spiritual dimension to life and, though agnostic, he believed that all life is sacred. He viewed all nature with awe and wonder, ever seeking to probe through to a unifying centre to all existence.

A fundamental principle of his teaching was that one's own life and one's spiritual integrity are of more value than any object or function to which a person may devote himself. Teaching the need to be free and unfettered, he realized that the only freedom worth having is a freedom which results from perfect harmony with that power or principle which lies at the heart of all that is, and which he called TAO.

To understand Chuang-tzŭ's position we need to look at Confucianism, the dominant philosophy of his day. The Confucians taught that it is in a context of social relationships, responsibilities and obligations that individual personality is developed and the character of the *chun-tzŭ* or noble-minded man is formed. The wise man seeks for harmony in relationships. To do this he must make a conscious and persistent effort to pursue the Way or Tao which was followed by the sages of olden time. This consists in practising the four cardinal virtues of love, righteousness, propriety and wisdom. This seemed to be an excellent philosophy of life, but Confucianism had come to lay such strong emphasis on political, social and family responsibilities that there had gradually been built up a complex and artificial structure of rituals, duties, and orders of precedence. Every man, woman and child in family and state had his or her appropriate station in a complex nexus of relationships. Chuang-tzŭ realized that this system was stultifying the natural and creative impulses in man. He rebelled against it. He attacked it with humour and satire. He was convinced that to set up external standards of what is good and right is in danger of inhibiting the free and creative activity which is the noblest expression of the human spirit.

Chuang-tzŭ saw that all life is in a state of transition, never quite the same for one moment, constantly demanding a creative response. The Confucians taught a Way or Tao, but their Way was not the supreme Way. It was based on traditional wisdom, handed down from age to age. It was not the Way of Heaven but a human way, laid down in meticulous detail for all to follow. It fettered men, imposing external standards of conduct, inhibiting freedom to live and act as conscience dictated. Surely there was a higher Way than that of the Confucians, a Way greater than heaven and earth, mysterious, timeless, ineffable; an eternal principle which gives to all things their form and substance, which makes them what they are, and leads them forward to what they are becoming; a Way above and beyond all existing phenomena. This Way cannot be grasped by the intellect, nor arrived at by rational discourse, argument or logic, nor defined in speech. The mysticism of Chuang-tzŭ grew out of a longing for and a persistent search after union with that Way. Only thus, he believed, can the individual hope to attain to that serenity and inner peace which is life indeed.

Confucius had had much to say about 'goodness' *(jên)*, and the need for those in authority to guide and restrain the people by moral force. For him there was no higher principle than to follow the Golden Rule: 'Treat others as you wish to be treated, and do to others the good which is good for oneself'. But what is good for oneself? That is a question which Chuang-tzŭ sought to answer. His search led him to conclusions very different from those accepted by the Confucians. Goodness, he believed, is not something outside oneself which one must strive to attain. In human life, as in the natural world, there are no absolute norms of virtue, justice or happiness applicable at all times and in all circumstances. What is one man's meat is another man's poison. He abhorred the idea that it is possible to set up standards and impose them on all men. To a person looking at Mrs Toad she might appear ugly and repellant, but to Mr Toad she is an object of desire. The long legs of a crane are well adapted to its needs as are the short legs of a duck. It would be absurd to think that one is doing good by trying to make them all equal in length. The conscious striving after moral excellence, the accumulation of virtue and merit are just as useless and ephemeral as are the strivings after power, glory, wealth or fame. All are a delusion.

As Chuang-tzŭ contemplated the world of nature in all its kaleidoscopic forms, and as he pondered on the varieties of human experience, he came to realize that the whole universe consists of a natural and spontaneous process of transition and change. Let one, therefore, attune oneself to

the rhythm of life which goes on unceasingly. Rid
self of all fretfulness, anxiety and conscious striving. Admit that all human experiences are fleeting
and temporary, and will only be resolved by
learning conformity with the Tao of one's own
nature. Only thus can the individual find that
peace and contentment which are indescribable.

Chuang-tzǔ certainly believed that there is an
eternal principle which lies within and beyond all
that exists. What it is in itself remains a supreme
mystery. But he believed that wisdom lay in seeking for it in the inmost of one's own mind, in a
quietude beyond conceptual thought or reasoning.
In what he called 'a fast of the mind' it is possible
to reach through to an ecstatic union, and allow
Tao to exert unimpeded action within one's own
nature. This is, perhaps, what he means by 'non-
activity' or 'not-doing' (wu wei), a spontaneous
action without thought of result. Because virtue,
happiness and the good life are not to be found by
conscious striving, the professional recluse is just
as wide of the mark as the Confucian in his self-
conscious striving after perfection. There is only
one Absolute, whether of truth, beauty or goodness, and that is in Tao. Therefore the truly wise
and great learn to rest themselves in Tao.

THE TAO-TÊ-CHING

The book of Lao-tzǔ, later to be known as the
Tao-Tê-Ching, has all the appearances of being
composed by some unknown Taoist about the
year 240 B.C. It is a subtle and clever polemical

work aimed at controverting the teachings of Confucians and Legalists. The traditional view that it is the work of Lao-tzŭ, an older contemporary of Confucius, is no longer tenable. All attempts to validate the historicity of Lao-tzŭ have failed. The earliest accounts concerning him are the result of confusing a recluse named Li-erh of the Warring States period with a legendary Lao-tan or Lao-lai-tzŭ who is supposed to have lived for more than 160 years and finally disappeared into the unknown through a western frontier post. We are informed that Li-erh taught a doctrine of self-effacement and namelessness.

The *Tao-Tê-Ching* is an anthology of Taoist wisdom designed to exert a practical impact on political and social theory. Towards the end of the third century B.C. there were ominous signs of the absolute state control which led to the totalitarianism imposed by the first emperor of China. (221–209 B.C.) The author witnessed the gradual disintegration of society as scholar-statesmen applied one panacea after another. In the state of Ch'in the regimentation of the people for food production and war under harsh penal laws was producing what was virtually a slave-state. He believed that there was a better way, a way that would give life, hope and happiness to the people. In seeking material for his work he turned to the wise teachings of Taoist philosophers and mystics which were in harmony with his own thinking. These teachings he skilfully incorporated into a short treatise which he ascribed to Lao-tzŭ (which, literally translated, means 'old

13

philosophers'). This little book has deservedly gained the reputation of being one of the world's greatest classics of mysticism, a reputation due entirely to the skill of its unknown compiler.

The author, being a man of his time, could envisage no other political system than that of absolute monarchy. He preached that the only ruler fitted to reign over a united kingdom was one who was distinguished by 'sageliness within the kingliness without'. The ideal monarch was one who lived his life in conformity with Tao. Acting thus he would only need to remain comparatively passive at the centre of his kingdom, in the same way as Tao is the quiescent pivot round which the whole activity of the universe revolves. The efficacy or power *(Tê)* of his own nature would flow out spontaneously even to the remotest districts influencing the lives of his people for good, and bringing contentment and happiness. There would be no need for new laws to restrain the people and coerce them to do his will. The proliferation of laws is a sure sign that things are wrong.

Like the Confucians, the author of the *Tao-Tê-Ching* looks back to a Golden Age in the far distant past, but he believed that the glorious achievements of the rulers of old were due to a wisdom which allows everything to follow its natural course.

> Those who in olden times gained the
> adherence of all did so by
> non-interference. If they had interfered
> they would not have gained this
> adherence.

14

This short treatise had a remarkable influence on Chinese theories of government throughout the whole period of the Chinese monarchy. Many of the emperors accepted and actively practised Taoism. Some of them became intensely interested in those techniques which were designed to promote longevity and offer the reward of immortality. Some became the dupes of Taoist adepts who engaged in alchemy and magic. But the best of them sought to model their lives and conduct on the teachings of Chuang-tzŭ and the *Tao-Tê-Ching*, and to find in Taoist wisdom a solution to the difficult problem of governing a large empire.

TAO

Fundamental to the teaching of all the great Taoist mystics is their concept of Tao, usually translated as the 'Way', but with a meaning far more significant than that term suggests. The original meaning of the Chinese character is that of a road, a path, a way. By extension it came to mean the way in which a person acts, the method he uses, the principle which directs what he does. Confucius used the term in this sense, but taught that the Way men ought to follow is the Way of the ancient rulers who modelled their conduct on the Way of Heaven. Thus they brought peace and welfare to their people. The true Way is therefore the Way of right conduct, to strive to act as heaven had ordained for mankind. The Taoist mystics gave a far deeper significance to Tao. As the Way followed by human societies was out of harmony with the Way of Heaven, and conducive of strife, disharmony and the growth of great evils, they sought only the Way of Heaven or Nature. Seeing that everything, themselves included, is in a state of perpetual transition and change, they concluded that nothing observable is permanent. Nothing has a self-hood of its own. All is in process, never remaining the same for one moment. They thrilled to the great cosmic scheme of things in which the smallest and least significant has its place. They realized that everything is intertwined and interdependent. Birth, growth, decay and death are all part of the same process. The decay and death of one thing means growth and life for another. They were content to accept their own involvement in this great cosmic movement. But what lay behind it all?

Taoist mysticism was born of a vision that, though everything observable by the human senses, even those senses themselves and the mind or spirit which controls them and seems to be so real in itself, all are contained in one all-embracing principle. To that principle they gave the name Tao. It seemed to them to be the most appropriate Chinese character, not in any sense to define but rather to indicate what they believed to be the only reality in the universe. It is the only thing that can be said to be 'self-so'. Though called Tao, it is nameless, beyond the comprehension of the human mind, only to be apprehended in quiet periods of ecstatic vision.

So, to these Taoist mystics Tao is the reality which gives to all phenomena their form and substance. It is unchanging, invisible and eternal, a unity which lies at the heart of a universal flux. It is beyond both 'being' and 'non being', resting in an absolute stillness. The whole universe is essentially One, and the wise man realizes his own indissoluble unity with the whole. By reaching down into the Tao of his own nature he hopes to attain a perfect oneness with the principle of all life and movement. In such tranquillity nothing can ever disturb the spirit which realizes that joy and sorrow, life and death, are but incidental to the marvellous ordering of things, and are no more significant than night and day.

Some Western scholars made the mistake of translating Tao as 'God'. The orthodox idea of God in Christianity is far from the Taoist concept of Tao. The personal, creative and redemptive God of Christian theology is quite alien from Taoist thought. Tao is represented as being devoid of action, thought, feeling and desire. It is non-purposive. Moreover, the Christian idea that man holds a special relationship with God is regarded as absurd by Taoist mystics. Chuang-tzŭ believed that man holds no closer relation to the ultimate principle of the universe than does such a lowly insect as the ant, or panic grass, or even such seemingly inanimate objects as an earthenware tile or a lump of manure. From the standpoint of Tao all things are of equal worth, and though to have attained to the human form is a source of joy, a man's life on earth is only a fleeting moment in an eternal process of transformation in which there are myriad forms equally good.

Tao does not exist in the same way as things exist. The mystics spoke of Tao as 'non-being' *(wu)*. By non-being they did not mean nothingness. Out of non-being all things that have being emerged. Tao may even be regarded as having 'being' since the whole universe depends upon it for its existence. It is the mysterious mother which rears and nurtures all phenomena. It is the great unity, the progenitor of heaven and earth and all things.

Two modalities within Tao are in constant interplay, and are known as *yin* and *yang*. The theory of yin and yang was well known to the Taoist mystics and accepted by them. Yin and yang were regarded as the agents of that perpetual transformation which goes on within everything; two equal and opposite forces, one quiescent, the other active. They acted together in complete harmony. Light and shade, summer and winter, day and night, heat and cold, male and female; all that is was explained as resulting from the interaction and interpenetration of these two forces. Nothing could be described as entirely yang or yin. In the processes of change yang or yin might be in the ascendant, but an inevitable reversal took place. Thus, when yang reaches its apogee at the summer solstice yin is already beginning to take over the ascendancy.

This dualism, which is but an expression of a primal unity, influenced all schools of Chinese thought. It is very different from the dualism found, for instance, in Zoroastrianism, and which influenced Christianity. There Ormuzd and

Arihman represent conflicting powers of good and evil, truth and lies, spiritual light and darkness. They are opposed, intent on the destruction of their opposite. For the Taoist mystic yang and yin are modalities of Tao independent of any idea of morality. They sustain an evolving process in complete harmony and are complementary to one another. Everything in the universe finds its origin, its completion and its unity with everything else in Tao.

TÊ

Tê is the efficacy, power or vital force of Tao; that which gives to a thing its form and character and its potentiality to become. Tê is usually translated 'virtue', but this can be misleading. For Tê is not virtue as opposed to vice, but rather an inner quality of character which is powerfully effective in influencing others and moulding events without conscious effort.

The Taoist mystics believed that in stillness of the mind, in a trance-like state, oblivious of the outside world, they could release within themselves a vital energy (Tê) which would prove more effective than any conscious, deliberate or willed action. While the Confucians taught that all men should consciously cultivate their Tê, the Taoist claimed that Tê is the spontaneous unfolding of the Tao of their own nature. A man exercises his Tê by being his true self.

It is because of the quality of their Tê that great sages and wise kings differ from other men and are able by force of character alone to wield great influence. This is clearly brought out in the twelfth chapter of Chuang-tzŭ where it says:

> The princely man finds his source in Tê
> . . . In deep antiquity the rulers
> governed the world without action,
> simply by the exercise of heavenly Tê.

Chuang-tzŭ goes on to say that the man in possession of kingly Tê is able to see light in total darkness, find harmonies in utter silence, penetrate to the spiritual essence of things. So, seemingly inactive and even vacuous, he meets the needs of all who seek his help.

THE TAOIST MYSTIC WAY

The Taoist mystics, in their pursuit of the ultimate goal of oneness with Tao, followed two distinct methods of gaining mystical insight. In the first place, they became absorbed in the wonders and mysterious adaptations of nature. They took delight in the contemplation of the world around them, and in quietude came to an ecstatic vision of that which they believed to be the essence of all being and all action. In the second place, they practised deep introspection, seeking to uncover the roots of their own nature.

Taoist mysticism has sometimes been contrasted with Christian mysticism as being agnostic, atheistic, or essentially a nature mysticism. It has been criticized as being pantheistic, akin to what we find in the writings of Richard Jefferies or in some of the poems of Wordsworth. The emphasis is on spontaneity and naturalism, on process rather than being, on the inter-relatedness and fundamental unity of all things in Tao. There is no emphasis on the distinctiveness of individual self-hood. Myriad forms of life emerge only to return to a primal non-being in Tao before entering again into some form of being. Thus nature appears to the Taoists as a rhythmic pulsation, ever changing and transforming, coming to birth and dying. Wisdom consists in learning conformity to this universal rhythm.

The wise man seeks to return to his own root. This is done by 'fasting and emptying the mind', by 'sitting in forgetfulness', by learning a stillness of all faculties till thoughts and feelings are obliterated. A wise man is like 'an unweaned child', nourishing himself on Tao as an infant draws nourishment from its mother's breast. He is 'a deep valley', an 'empty vessel', receptive to all that flows into it. He resembles an uncarved block of marble which contains all the potentialities to become what a supreme artist has in mind for it. This 'returning to the root' is accomplished by emptying the mind of all desire, for desire feeds on itself, and leads to an accumulation of more and more things. Even a craving for knowledge must be resisted, for learning only leads to filling the mind, whereas the follower of Tao subtracts day by day, not adding but decreasing until he finally reaches non-action and an emptiness which Tao alone can fill.

It is by non-interference that all is naturally accomplished. 'The sage does nothing, yet achieves everything.' By blunting his senses and attaining to an absolute stillness of the mind, the Taoist mystic gains a perfect equilibrium. By returning to the root of his being the Taoist sage acts as a catalyst so that all who come into contact with him are transformed, in the same way as Tao, the quiescent centre of the universe has power over all phenomena. There is no longer any need to rely on laws or ordinances, taboos and prohibitions in order to rule men's lives. The mystic power of Tê brings all things to a Grand Conformity.

Chuang-tzŭ and the other great Taoist mystics needed no other techniques to assist them to return to the root, hold fast to the unity, and realize their oneness with Tao. But some Taoists sought to induce mystical experience by means of a kind of yoga, self-hypnosis, rhythmic dancing, strict dieting and drugs. As time went on these practices became very common, and more and more Taoists made the search for immortality their chief aim.

LATER DEVELOPMENTS IN TAOIST MYSTICISM

By the early centuries of the Christian era Taoism in China was developing both as a profound mystical philosophy which attracted many Confucians, and as an institutional religion which, by interpenetration with Buddhism, became a popular or folk religion of the common people. Over the centuries there developed a huge corpus of Taoist literature, known as the *Tao Tsang*, much of its contents being esoteric, vaguely understood except by Taoist Masters who gave their lives to its study. By the third and fourth centuries A.D. schools of neo-Taoism arose, influenced by the writings of Wang-pi (A.D. 226–249); Hsiang-hsiu (c. A.D. 221–300) noted for his great commentary of *Chuang-tzŭ*; Kuo-hsiang (d. A.D. 312); and Ko-hung (c. A.D. 268–334) who found in Taoism a philosophical basis for his alchemistic search after an elixir of immortality and wrote a monumental work on the art of becoming an immortal. The movement known as *hsüan-hsüeh* or 'dark and mysterious learning' had a great influence. Numerous groups of Taoist scholars engaged in what they called *ch'ing-t'an* or 'pure conversations'. They sought an unconventional and carefree way of life, living according to nature, seeking freedom and self-realization and turning their backs on worldly advantage. In an extreme form this movement towards unconventionality is exemplified in the Seven Sages of the Bamboo Grove (third century A.D.). These seven friends abandoned themselves to a carefree life, communing with nature, writing and reciting poetry, drinking wine, playing the lute and engaging in 'pure conversations' which only ended when they reached a glorious indifference to the world and intimacy with Tao. Then they 'stopped talking and silently understood each other with a smile'.

Through the centuries religious Taoism founded many great monasteries, modelled on those of Buddhism, where the contemplative life was cultivated and the works of Chuang-tzŭ and Lao-tzŭ studied. Often a monk would leave the confines of the monastery to become a hermit, solely intent on inner perfection and union with Tao. The teachings of the Taoist mystics also exerted a great influence on the lives of men and women in all ranks of society, whereby the moralistic rigidities of Confucianism were counterbalanced by a free, joyous acceptance of life as it is, a sensitivity to the beauties of nature, and a belief in the fundamental unity of all under heaven. Taoist mysticism contributed to a Chinese form of Buddhism known as *Ch'an* (in Japanese, Zen), which enriched the cultural and religious life of China, Korea, Japan and Vietnam. The writings, the poetry and the paintings of the Zen masters encourage belief in a reality which no intellectual probing can uncover.

In the following collection of sayings and stories I have included some familiar passages which, because of their worth and beauty, their mystical and poetical insight, and their relevance to our present-day condition, deserve a place in any anthology of Taoist mysticism. Many of the other sayings and stories will, I trust, be unfamiliar to the general reader. Though relying mainly on Chuang-tzŭ and the Tao-Tê-Ching, I have incorporated extracts from a wide spectrum of Taoist mystical writings.

STORIES AND SAYINGS

★ I ★

BEFORE HEAVEN AND EARTH came
forth there was something formless yet complete. How silent! How still! Standing alone and
unchanging, all-pervasive and unwearying, it may
be regarded as the mother of all things. I do not
know its name but, if forced to give it a name, I
would call it 'TAO'. Forced to designate it, I
would call it 'great'. So great is it that it may be
said to go on and on, so far that it turns back on
itself.

★ II ★

TAO is the origin of all things. It is that by which
all things come to their completion. By it all
things exist.

★ III ★

TAO is that which fills all forms, yet man is not
able to hold it secure. It departs but does not
return. It arrives but does not abide. Desire it and
you do not so much as hear a sound of it. Yet
suddenly it is found within the mind. So obscure
is it that its form cannot be seen. So pervasive is it
that it is within all our being. One cannot see its
action nor hear its sound, and yet it brings to perfection whatever it seeks to accomplish. Such we
call Tao.

THAT which can be thought of as Tao (lit. Tao that can be tao'd) is not the absolute Tao. Whatever name that can be applied to it is not its absolute name. Nameless, it is the source of heaven and earth. Named, it is the mother of all things. Therefore, considered as absolute 'non-being' we desire to see into its mystery; as absolute 'being' we desire to observe its delimitations. These two (non-being and being), though identical in origin, emerge under different names. Their common identity is called mysterious, mystery of mysteries, the gate of all mystery.

TAO is the origin of heaven and earth, and by it they are regulated. It existed before they were brought to completion, and no one has seen its form nor knows its name. It is called 'spiritual intelligence'.

THE outward manifestations of great power proceed only from Tao. Considered as a thing, Tao is vague and obscure, yet it lies within all forms and entities. How profound and unfathomable it is! Yet within it there is an essence, an essence which is very real. Within it lies its own verification. From ancient times down to the present day the fame of it remains. It may be called the father of all things.

★ VII ★

HOW great Tao flows along with the current! It can spread to the left or to the right. All things depend upon it for life and it does not reject them. Having completed a task, it does not rest there. It clothes all things but does not act as their overlord. So it is that, being without desire, it might be called insignificant. Yet all things revert to it without knowing that it is their overlord. It can be named among the greatest. It is able to succeed in being great because it never magnifies itself.

★ VIII ★

TAO is like a vessel which, though used, is never filled. How fathomless it is! As if it were the progenitor of all that exists! How deep it is! As if it were everlasting!

★ IX ★

TAO is like the ocean into which one can throw quantities of gold and silver and they disappear; into which can be thrown mountains of filth, and it is lost to sight. Tiny shrimps and great whales alike swim in its waters. All the rivers flow into it, yet it does not overflow. From its waters all beings are supplied and yet there is abundance for all.

TAO enfolds heaven and earth, binds the universe in place, contains the yin and the yang, rules over the three luminaries, and engages in inexhaustible activity.

TUNG-KUO-TZŬ asked Chuang-tzŭ: What is it that men call Tao? Where is it? Chuang-tzŭ replied: There is no place where it does not exist. Tung-kuo-tzŭ said: Be more specific. Chuang-tzŭ said: It is in an ant. How can it be so low? It is in the panic grass. But that is still lower. How is it possible? It is in an earthenware tile. It surely could not be lower than that! It is in excrement. Tung-kuo-tzŭ made no reply. Chuang-tzŭ said: Your question is not sufficiently apposite. When the inspector Huo asked the market super-intendent to test the fatness of a pig by pressing it with his foot, the further down he pressed and the more clearly he could decide. Now you think of Tao as being in a certain place, but it is not absent from anything. Such is perfect Tao according to my teaching; comprehensive, omnipresent, all-inclusive; these three different words all have a similar meaning. They all indicate the same Reality.

WHAT is meant by Tao? There is the Tao of men

and the Tao of nature. That which is venerated in inaction is the Tao of nature. That which is implicated in activity is called the Tao of men. The Tao of nature is chief; the Tao of men is subordinate. They are mutually far apart. This is something that we cannot but ponder over.

★XIII★

TAO always remains inactive, and yet there is nothing that it does not accomplish.

★XIV★

REVERSAL is the movement of Tao. Weakness is the practice of Tao. Everything is produced from Being, and Being is born of Non-Being.

★XV★

TAO brings things to birth and by its power they are nourished. Substance gives them form and environmental influences bring them to completion. This is the reason why among all phenomena there are none that do not honour Tao and esteem its efficacy. This honouring of Tao and esteeming its efficacy is not something that is forced, but it arises spontaneously. Therefore Tao gives them birth, and its power nourishes them, makes them grow, rears them, shelters them, brings them to maturity, protects them and covers them. What is called 'mysterious power' does not possess what it produces, does not rely on what it does, does not control what it presides over.

★XVI★

TAO is the household shrine of the universe. It is the treasure of the good, and the refuge of those who are not so good. Why is it that the men of old esteemed Tao so highly? Did they not say: Seek it and you will find it, and even your failings will be excused? So it was that they considered it to be of all things the most precious.

★XVII★

CHUANG-TZǓ said: To know Tao is easy. To refrain from talking about it is difficult. To know and not to speak appertains to nature. To know and to talk about what one knows appertains to the human. It was the natural rather than the human to which the men of old time sought to conform themselves. The knowledge of the petty man never gets away from such things as sending and receiving gifts and letters. He wears out his vital spirit on what is useless and trivial. Nevertheless, he longs to assist in guiding affairs and bringing form and formlessness into a great unity. Such a man is confused by the complexity of forms in the universe, for he has no understanding of the Great Beginning. The perfected man, on the other hand, allows his essential spirit to return to the beginningless, and blissfully closes his eyes in the region of non-being. His spirit is formless

30

like flowing water, bubbling forth in perfect purity. How pitiable are those who have an infinitesimal understanding and no comprehension of the Great Tranquillity!

FORMLESS becoming form; form becoming formless; this is something that all men know. It is not something that those who have attained to Tao regard as fundamental. It is something that all men discuss, but he who has attained to Tao does not discuss it. For discussion of it indicates that one has not attained. It is not grasped by clear-sightedness, and discussion of it is not so good as silence. Tao cannot be heard. To close one's ears is better than listening. This is called the Great Attainment.

ONLY WHEN that which has form resembles the formless will it be absolutely at peace. [Tao] issues from no source and enters through no aperture. Possessing reality, it is without an abiding place. Ever abiding, it is without end or beginning. It is timeless. All things have life and death. They issue forth and enter in. The manner of their emergence and departure is unseen, but we call it 'the gate of Nature'. The gate of Nature is non-being. Being cannot create being out of being. It must come forth out of non-being, and non-being is uniformly non-being in which the sage hides himself.

31

The wisdom of the ancients had its limits. What were those limits? There were men who thought that things always existed, complete, entire, so that nothing could be added. Then there were those who thought that things exist, but that life is loss and death a return, and that these states are separate. Again there were those who said that in the beginning there was non-being. Then came life for a short time, and then death. They considered non-being to be the head, life the body and death the rump. Whoever maintains that being and non-being, life and death, are one: I will be his friend!

★XX★

THAT by means of which all things are brought to birth is the (cosmic) essence. On earth below it produces the five cereals, and in heaven above the host of stars. It forms the spiritual beings betwixt earth and heaven. He who possesses it within the breast may be called a sage.

★XXI★

HE who has no clear understanding of Nature will not be pure in virtue. He who has no thorough understanding of Tao will find himself incapable. He who has no clear understanding of Tao is truly pitiable.

★XXII★

NO-BEGINNING said: Tao cannot be heard.

Heard, it is not Tao. Tao cannot be seen. Seen, it is not Tao. Tao cannot be described. Described, it is not Tao. That which knows what constitutes form is itself formless. There is no name to fit Tao. He who when asked about Tao gives an answer does not understand Tao, and even if one asks about Tao he will not hear about it. Tao cannot be inquired into, and if it is there will no answer. To ask about what cannot be asked is asking the impossible. To force an answer when there is no answer is to be inwardly lacking. One who is inwardly lacking attending on one who asks the impossible is like a man who does not perceive the cosmos outside nor understand the Great Source within. Such a one could never cross the Kun-lun mountain range nor wander in the Great Void.

★ XXIII ★

THAT which causes things to be things is not itself a thing. The limit of each thing is called its boundary. The unlimited lies within the limited, and though recognized within the limited it is, nevertheless, unlimited. We talk of fullness and emptiness, of withering and decay. It is Tao which makes things full or empty, but Tao itself is neither full nor empty. It is Tao which causes things to wither and decay, but it does not itself wither or decay. It is Tao which gives to things their beginning and end, but it itself has no beginning nor end. It is Tao which cases things to store up or disperse, but it itself neither stores up nor disperses.

THE most difficult tasks in the world should be performed when they are still easy. The greatest projects should be dealt with while they are still small. On this principle, the sage never tackles things when they have become great, and so he achieves greatness. Many difficulties are encountered when men treat hard things as easy. So it is that the sage, by treating easy things as though they were difficult, ends by finding nothing difficult.

★ XXV ★

THE principles of harmony and music were born of the supreme Unity, which produced the 'yin' and the 'yang', and these separate only to unite again and they unite only to separate. This process is called 'the rule of heaven'.

★ XXVI ★

IN UNITY is the origin of the life-force. Movement within this life-force produces purpose. Enfolded upon itself it is called 'chaos', but when chaos opened up the four seasons revolved and all things were produced.

★ XXVII ★

IN THE BEGINNING, before yet there were heaven and earth, there were only 'idea' and 'form'. Dark and mysterious, the beginnings are unknown. Two spiritual forces, inextricably mingled, came to birth and they completed heaven and earth. They were separated as yin and yang, and divided off the confines of the universe. The yielding and the unyielding were complementary to each other, and all things received their form. The grosser elements formed animals and the finer elements composed man. Hence man received from heaven his spiritual nature and from earth his material frame. At death the spiritual and the material each returns to its origin, and the 'self' no longer subsists. Therefore the sage, in following his desires, models himself on heaven, and is neither held in thrall by material things nor led astray by men. For he looks upon heaven as his father, and on earth as his mother. The movements of yin and yang are his law, and his life is regulated by the four seasons. His purity is found in the serenity of heaven and his peace in the stability of earth. When things lose these, they die, and when they obey them, they live. It is in the serene expanse of heaven that the intelligent spirits have their dwelling-place. It is in the void of negation that the Tao makes its abode. Therefore, whoever searches for Tao outside of himself loses it within. Whoever seeks to retain it within loses it without.

XXVIII

AT the birth of all men heaven provides the essence and earth provides the form. The union of

35

these two constituents produces man. If they harmonize, he is born. If they do not harmonize, he is not born.

★XXIX★

THE PRACTICE of learning brings daily addition. The practice of Tao brings daily subtraction. One subtracts and subtracts until one finally rests in inactivity. Through non-activity all is achieved.

★XXX★

THE EMOTIONS of love and hate bring trouble to the mind and daily exhaust the spirit. The reason why a man fails to reach the destined term of his life is because he lives life at too fast a pace. Heaven and earth revolve in mutual interplay and all phenomena are but one whole. If you know this unity then you know all that needs to be known. This 'self' is but a thing, just as things are things. The creator brought me to birth and will destroy me as if I were a lump of clay. While living I am but a slave, and when I am dead I shall be at rest. As a living man I have a body seven [Chinese] feet high. When I am dead I shall have enough space for my coffin. During life I shall be like all things that have form. When I am dead I shall be engulfed in formlessness.

★XXXI★

THE REASON why men do not attain to immortality is because they destroy that within themselves which is invisible, and dissipate that which is immaterial. So they are unable to cause their material body to unite with the Real. Hence they die.

★XXXII★

THAT which brings the living to birth itself never dies. That which transforms all things is not itself subject to change. Before a man is born he becomes one with the principle of change. Death and life are one, and on death a man returns to the source of all things. If one knows the happiness of being unborn he will not fear death. The perfect man leans upon a pillar which cannot be uprooted, and learns from a teacher which never dies.

★XXXIII★

THE CREATOR deals with things as a potter does with his clay. He takes a lump of clay and makes a vessel, and vessels which he has already made he squashes back again into a formless lump. Those who dwell on the banks of a river draw the waters to irrigate their gardens. The water does not complain as to whether it is in the river or on the gardens. So the sage is content with his situation and rejoices in his appointed lot.

★XXXIV★

THE LIFE of man between heaven and earth is like

a sunbeam passing a crack in a wall. In a moment it is ended. Flowing forth with a sudden start, there are none that do not emerge (out of non-being). Slipping and gliding away, there are none that do not return. A transformation, and they are born. Again a transformation, and they are dead. Living things grieve over this and mankind mourns. But is it not a loosening of one's natural bow-case, letting fall away one's natural wrappings, an adjustment, a mutation by which the animal soul and the spirit depart, followed by the body, and then at length the great reversion?

* XXXV *

WHEN YEN-HUI asked about the 'fast of the mind', Confucius replied: Your will must be unified. Cease listening with your ears and listen with the mind. Cease listening with the mind and listen with the vital spirit. It is for ears to hear; it is for the mind to cogitate; but as for the vital spirit, it is empty and receptive of all things. Tao can only rest in vacuity. To empty the mind is indeed 'the fast of the mind'.

* XXXVI *

COCKS crow, dogs bark; this is something that everyone understands. But even with great understanding one is not able to explain how they become what they are. Even more, one can have no idea as to what they will become. One may analyse things that are so tiny as to be insignificant and indistinguishable, so large that it is impossible to enclose them. Whether there is something that causes them to be, or whether nothing makes them so, one cannot get away from 'thinghood', and one ends up in error. If something causes a thing to be, it is substantial. If nothing makes it, it is insubstantial. Name and substance appertain to a thing's reality. Namelessness and insubstantiality appertain to its unreality. One can talk and one can think about this, but the more one talks and the further one gets from it. Before it is born a thing cannot avoid being born. After death it cannot hinder death. But death and life are not far apart. The reason for them cannot be seen. Whether things have a cause or not is doubtful. I look for their origin, but they issue forth endlessly. I search for their ending, but they continue unceasingly. Inexhaustible, unending, the same principle which applies to things applies also to talk about them. Perhaps the origin of words has a cause or does not have a cause, ending and beginning like things?

★XXXVII★

THE WEAKEST thing in the world is more powerful than the hardest. Though not having substance it is able to penetrate, entering by means of spacelessness. From this I know the value of non-action. In the whole world there are very few people who attain to teaching without words and bringing benefit without action.

★ XXXVIII ★

HE who knows Tao is sure to be familiar with basic principles. He who is familiar with basic principles is sure to have a clear understanding of circumstances. Having a clear understanding of circumstances he will not allow anything to harm him. Being perfect in virtue, fire cannot burn him, water cannot drown him, cold and heat cannot harm him, birds and beasts cannot injure him. That is not to say that he makes light of these things, but he discriminates between what is safe and what is dangerous. He remains tranquil in affliction or in happiness. He is cautious in his goings out and comings in. So there is nothing that can do him harm. Hence the saying, 'What pertains to Nature is internal, what pertains to the human is external'. Virtue resides in what is natural. When a man has understanding of what activities appertain to the natural and to the human, he roots himself in the natural, and takes his stand in virtue. So he will go forward or backward, extend or contract, revert to the essential or speak of the absolute.

★ XXXIX ★

GREAT rivers and seas are able to act as kings over the numerous valleys because of their aptitude for being lower than they. That is why they are able to act as kings over the numerous valleys. Therefore the sage who desires to be above the people must speak as though he were lower than they. In order to lead them he must place himself behind them, and so, though the place of a sage is above, the people do not feel his weight. The people are not harmed by his leadership, and so all men rejoice to honour him and do not reject him. Because he does not contend there is no one in the empire who can contend with him.

★ XL ★

THE SAGE, though he puts himself behind, comes to the fore. Though he puts himself outside, he remains safe. Is it not because of his impartiality that he is able to bring to perfection his own personal preference?

★ XLI ★

HE who has a clear understanding of the virtues of heaven and earth may be called 'Great Source', 'Great Ancestor'. Being in harmony with heaven he is able to harmonize all under heaven and to be in accord with all men. To be in accord with men is called human joy. To be in accord with heaven is called heavenly joy.

★ XLII ★

CHUANG-TZǓ said: Oh what a teacher is mine! O what a teacher is mine! It brings all things into order but does not consider itself to be oppressive. Its favours extend to ten thousand generations but it does not consider itself to be benevolent. Old as antiquity it does not consider itself to be long-lived. Sustaining heaven and earth, it fashions the form of things but does not consider itself to be skilled. This is what is called heavenly joy! Therefore it is said that for the man who knows the joy of heaven, his life is motivated by heaven and his death is a transformation of his substance. In quietude he shares the efficacy of yin. In activity he flows along with yang. Thus he who knows the joy of heaven does not incur the displeasure of heaven, nor the opposition of men, nor entanglement with things, nor the disapproval of spiritual beings. Hence it is said that his motivation is of heaven and his quiescence is of earth. Settled in singleness of mind, he rules over the world. His animal spirit is not harmed. His ethereal spirit is not exhausted. Settled in singleness of mind, all things submit to him. It could be said that his emptiness and stillness extend through heaven and earth, and penetrate all things. This is what is called the joy of heaven. This joy of heaven is that by which the mind of the sage cares for everything under heaven.

★XLIII★

IN ancient times those who excelled in following Tao had a thorough understanding of the mysterious and the profound. So profound were they that they cannot be understood. As they cannot be understood, I will do my best to describe their appearance. How well-prepared they were, like a person who crosses a stream in winter! How cautious they were, like a man who fears his neighbours on every side! How expansive, like ice beginning to melt! How open wide, like a valley! How murky, like muddy water! How can one clarify what is murky? Tranquilize it, and it will gradually become clear. How can one gain lasting repose? After activity, it will gradually ensue. Those who cherish Tao do not crave after fulfilment. As regards being unfulfilled, what matters is the capacity to wear out without being concerned about completion.

★XLIV★

THE SAGE cherishes unity, and he tests everything by it. He does not display himself and in consequence he is revealed. He does not assert himself, and so becomes clearly manifest. He is not boastful, and so he is successful. Lacking in self-esteem, he achieves leadership. Just because he does not contend, no one in the whole world can contend against him.

★XLV★

WITHOUT going out of doors one may come to possess extensive knowledge. Without looking through the window one may know the Way of Heaven. He who travels furthest knows least. Therefore the sage gets to his destination without travelling. He is illuminated without seeing. He brings things to completion without (purposive) action.

THE SAGE has no fixed mind of his own. He makes the mind of the people his own. I treat good people as good. I also treat bad people as good. In that way I obtain goodness. I trust trustworthy people. I also trust the untrustworthy. I thus obtain their trust.

★XLVII★

A wise man has said 'By my non-activity the people are themselves transformed. By my love of quietude the people are themselves rectified. Because of my undertaking nothing the people prosper. Being myself without desire the people are themselves naturally unspoilt.'

★XLVIII★

(ONE who attains Tao) stops his apertures and closes his gate (of perception). He blunts sharpness, unravels tangles, dims brightness and levels tracts. This is called 'mysterious levelling'. He cannot be moved by friendship or by indifference. He cannot be advantaged or harmed, honoured or humbled. That is why of all creatures he is held in highest esteem.

★XLIX★

THE WAY OF HEAVEN may be likened to the bending of a bow. What is high is brought down and what is low is elevated. Surplus is diminished and deficiency supplied. The Way of Heaven is to take from those who have more than enough and give to those who have an insufficiency. Man's way is very different. It is to deprive the deficient and offer more to the opulent. In the whole world where are they who are able to take from those who have a surplus and give more to the indigent? Only those who follow Tao. Therefore the sage does not presume on what he does, nor rest in his achievements. He has no desire to display his worthiness.

★ L ★

A TREE of great girth grew from a tiny sapling. A nine-storied tower began as a heap of earth. A journey of a thousand leagues started with a footstep. People engaged in affairs often ruin them just as they are about to complete them. If you don't want to ruin your affairs be as careful of the end as of the beginning. Therefore the sage desires to be without desire. He does not prize things that are difficult to obtain. He learns not to learn. He turns back to what all men pass by. Thus he upholds the spontaneity of all things and does not dare to act.

★ LI ★

YOU were born with a human form in which you take delight. But as regards the human form there are endless changes for it to undergo. Is not this a cause for supreme joy? So it is that the sage journeys among things that can never be lost but which ever abide. For his youth and his old age, his beginning and end, are all good. He serves as a model for all men. How much more should we model ourselves on that to which all things belong and on which the great transformation depends? Tao has reality and evidence, yet it is without action and without form. It is transmitted but cannot be appropriated. It is attainable but invisible. It was firmly established of old before heaven and earth existed. It gives spirituality to spirits and to the high gods. It gave birth to heaven and earth. Beyond the highest height, it is not regarded as lofty. Below the lowest depths, it is not regarded as deep. Before heaven and earth, it is not regarded as long-lasting. Earlier than antiquity, it is not regarded as old.

★ LII ★

THE SAGE embraces heaven and earth and his favour extends to all the world. Yet his lineage is not known. Therefore in life he holds no titles, and in death no posthumous honours. He does not accumulate material things, nor seek to establish his fame. Such may be called a Great Man.

★ LIII ★

IN ancient times the true man did not rebel against penury, was not ambitious to succeed, and did not scheme and plan. That being so, if he committed an error he did not make it a subject for vain regret. When he accomplished something he did not consider this achievement as anything special. And so, he would climb heights without fear, enter water without being soaked, and fire without being burnt. With knowledge such as his one could mount up to be with Tao.

THE SAGE observes nature but does not assist it. Though complete in virtue he does not accumulate it. Emanating from Tao he does not contrive plans. Being in accord with benevolence he does not presume upon it. Cleaving to justice he does not accumulate it. He accords with the rituals and does not shun their use. He takes affairs in hand and does not excuse himself. He orders things by law and allows no confusion. He depends upon people and does not make light of them. He relies on material things and does not discard them. As regards things, though none are fit for use, one cannot but use them.

AS REGARDS the quietude of the sage, he is not quiet because quietness is said to be good. He is quiet because the multitude of things cannot disturb his quietude. When water is still one's beard and eyebrows are reflected in it. A skilled carpenter uses it in a level to obtain a measurement. If still water is so clear, how much more are the mental faculties! The mind of a sage is the mirror

of heaven and earth in which all things are
reflected.

WIDE learning does not necessarily imply understanding. Eloquence does not necessarily imply
wisdom. The sage rejects such things. He holds
on to that which increases without adding to
one's gain, to that which diminishes without
adding to one's loss. It is deep and profound like
the ocean. Lofty and imposing, it ends only to
return to its beginning. It moves and measures all
things and does not fail them. Is not this something very different from your [Confucian] Tao?
That which all creatures come to rely on and
which does not fail them, is not this the real Tao?

HE who knows perfection does not seek, does not
lose, does not reject, and does not change because
of material things. He finds within himself inexhaustible resources, and following the ancient
ways he does not fret. Such is the sincerity of the
Great Man.

ALL existing things are really one. We regard
those that are beautiful and rare as valuable, and
those that are ugly as foul and rotten. The foul
and rotten may come to be transformed into what
is rare and valuable, and the rare and valuable into

what is foul and rotten. Therefore it is said that one vital energy pervades the world. Consequently, the sage values Oneness.

★ LIX ★

HEAVEN and earth possess great beauties but do not speak of them. The four seasons are governed by clear regulations but they do not discuss them. All created things have principles by which they are brought to completion, but they do not talk about them. The sage knows the reason for the beauties of heaven and earth, and comprehends the principle of all things, and that is why the perfect man remains inactive. The great sage does not act. He may be said to regard heaven and earth as his model. Now when the pure spiritual essence and the intelligence of heaven and earth unite with material things a hundred transformations take place.cThings are already alive or dead, square or round, and no one knows what brings this about. With its restless activity the whole of creation has been firmly established from ancient times. Vast as the universe is, it does not depart from its inmost self (Tao). The veriest trifle waits upon it to achieve bodily form. There is nothing in creation that does not suffer the ups and downs of fortune, unstable to the end of its days. Yin and yang and the four seasons move along, each in its appointed order. Obscure as if it did not exist, Tao abides. It flourishes without form, being only spirit, and creation is nourished by it without knowledge. It is called the original cause. Its presence can be observed within nature.

⋆ LX ⋆

GREAT WISDOM looks into what is both far off and near and, in consequence, considers that small things are not paltry nor great things too great. It recognizes that there is no end to the measurement of things. In verifying events both present and past, it is not over-concerned in regard to what happened long ago, nor does it stand on tip-toe to gather up the present, for it knows that time does not cease. It examines into the nature of fullness and emptiness, and so does not take pleasure in getting things, nor find sorrow in losing them, for it knows the inconstancy of one's lot in life. It has a clear understanding of the even road, and so does not rejoice in life nor regard death as a calamity. It knows that one's end and one's beginning cannot be determined.

⋆ LXI ⋆

THE BODY will wear out if it labours and takes no rest. One's spiritual essence will become fatigued and exhausted if it is used unceasingly. It is the nature of water to become clear if it is not stirred up. Do not move it and it remains placid. But if you dam it up so that its natural flow becomes interrupted it cannot become clear. It is a symbol of heavenly virtue. So one might say that to be simple and pure, unadulterated and unmixed, still, unified and unchanging, placid and inactive, moved only by natural action – this is the way to nourish the spirit. One's vital energy flows out in all directions. There is nowhere to which it does not extend. Above, it reaches to heaven. Below, it encircles the earth. It transforms and nurtures all things. Yet no representation of it is possible. Its fame is that of a supreme ruler. The way to purity is simply to guard well the spirit; to guard and not lose it. When the spirit is unified and one with the vital essence, a person is found to be in harmony with the heavenly order. A common saying puts the matter thus: all men prize profit; the honest official prizes fame; the worthy man esteems ambition; but the sage prizes his vital essence. Now as regards simplicity, the meaning is that it has nothing mixed with it. As regards purity, the meaning is that the spirit is not impaired. When a man is able to embody purity and simplicity we call him a True Man.

★LXII★

MAN's place in the universe is like that of a flea inside one's clothing, or like an ant in a hollow underground. The flea may jump about; the ant may creep and crawl; yet can the atmosphere of their hiding places be altered by these movements? Heaven indeed is vast, and man is very small. How can a man hope to influence the atmosphere of the heavens with his tiny body of seven [Chinese] feet? Hopeless, indeed, is such an ambition.

★LXIII★

HE who knows sufficiency will not weary himself

with thoughts of gain. He will take account of what he has, but will have no anxiety about losing it. He who practises the cultivation of his inner being will not be disconcerted because he lacks social standing.

★ LXIV ★

THIRTY spokes fit together into the hub of a wheel, and so the usefulness of a carriage depends upon what is non-existent (the hollow centre). Clay is moulded to make a hollow vessel, but the vessel's usefulness lies in its emptiness. A dwelling is made by cutting out doors and windows, and so the usefuless of a dwelling depends upon empty spaces. Thus, what exists is advantageous, and what does not exist has its use.

★ LXV ★

BETTER to stop short than to fill to overflowing. One cannot preserve for long the sharp edge of a sword. A hall filled with bronze and jade cannot be protected. Pride in wealth and status leads to calamity. It is Heaven's way to retire when its work is completed.

★ LXVI ★

THE highest excellence is like water. The excellence of water lies in its capacity to benefit all things without striving. Because of this it resembles Tao.

52

THE emotions of love and hate are harmful to the mind. It is the mind that rules over the body, and the treasure of the mind is the vital spirit. The sage prizes and honours it and dares not transgress. There is nothing from which he remains too aloof and nothing to which he grows too attached. He is obedient to Heaven and to Tao. His ethereal spirit *(hun)* and his animal soul *(p'o)* stay in their place of lodgement and his spiritual nature maintains its basic position.

YOU make distinctions between benevolence and justice, examine into the limits of similarity and difference, observe the alterations of movement and stillness, apply rules for giving and receiving, measure the emotions of liking and disliking, regulate the periods of joy and anger; and scarcely do you escape from harm. If you were diligent in cultivating your person, careful to hold on to your spirituality, gave up external things to others; then you would be without worry. To neglect the cultivation of oneself so as to seek things of other men, is not this superficial?

SPIRITUALITY is the acme of purity and sincerity. Without purity and sincerity you cannot move men. So it is that he who forces himself to weep, though he makes great lamentation, is not really sorry. He who forces himself to be angry, though he looks fierce, does not overawe. He who forces himself to be affectionate, though full of smiles, does not by his smiling produce harmony. True lamentation is soundless sorrow. True anger overawes without bursting forth. True affection needs no smiles to bring about harmony. Spirituality is inward, but it expresses itself externally. That is why spirituality is to be prized.

★ LXX ★

TAO is the cause of all things. They die if they lose it. They live if they obtain it. In the conduct of affairs to oppose it brings ruin, to obey it brings success. Therefore the sage venerates it wherever it abides. Now if it could be said of a simple fisherman that he possesses Tao, could I dare not to respect him?

★ LXXI ★

SAGES regard the accomplishments of emperors and kings as superfluous. They are not the means by which the personality is perfected and life cared for. The worldly gentlemen of the present day for the most part dissipate their lives in an ardent desire for things. Is not this pitiable? Whenever a sage acts he first examines into his circumstances and considers his course of action. Here, for example, is a man who would use the priceless pearl of the Marquis of Sui to shoot at a

sparrow eight thousand feet away. Ridiculous!
Why? Because he would use something of great
value in his desire to gain a trifle. Now this life of
ours, is it not itself of far greater value than the
pearl of the Marquis of Sui?

★ LXXII ★

WHEN Tao is practised by the individual its efficacy is genuine. Practised in the home, its efficacy
suffices. Practised in a neighbourhood, its efficacy
is outspreading. Practised in a state, its efficacy is
abundant. Practised in the empire, its efficacy is
universal. Therefore one should regard others as
one regards self, other families as one's own family, other neighbourhoods as one's own neighbourhood, other states as one's own state, the
whole empire as one's own empire. It is from this
that I know what really constitutes the empire.

★ LXXIII ★

IF ONE wishes to be contracted, one must first be
stretched. In order to become weak, one must
first be strong. Before one can dispense, one must
first prosper. Before one can take away, one must
first give. This is called subtle perspicacity. The
sage conquers what is hard, and the weak overcomes the strong.

★ LXXIV ★

A WISE MAN knows others. A clear-minded man
knows himself. A strong man masters others. A

truly powerful man masters himself.
It is riches to know when one has enough.
A resolute man goes forward forcefully.
A man will continue for a long time who does not lose his place in life.
It is long life to die and not to perish.

∗ LXXV ∗

A HUMAN personality is said to have two soul constituents. There is the ethereal soul (hun) and the animal soul (p'o). The ethereal soul is 'yang', pure and intelligent. The animal soul is 'yin', turbid and obscure. The true man nourishes his ethereal soul whilst common folks nourish their animal souls. . . . In a living man the two soul constituents live together in harmonious relationship like husband and wife. At death they separate. The ethereal soul rises and the animal soul descends, and so their relationship ceases.

∗ LXXVI ∗

IN the whole world there is nothing so soft and yielding as water, and yet nothing prevails better in attacking what is hard and strong. It is this quality of not being hard and strong which makes its task easy. The soft overcomes the hard. The weak overcomes the strong. In the whole world there are none who do not know this, and yet none are able to practise it. Therefore a sage has said: It is he who accepts the dirt of a state who is called lord over its altars. He who takes upon himself the evils of a state can become ruler over the whole land.

LAO-TAN said: Take care not to ruffle men's minds. The mind of man becomes depressed or elevated, imprisoned and destroyed. When the mind is mild and submissive it gently overcomes what is hard and strong as it quietly cuts and carves and polishes. Its heat is a blazing fire. Its cold is congealed ice. So swift is it that in the space of looking up and down it has twice roamed beyond the four seas. At rest it is profound and still. In activity, flying and floating about, it is restless and untameable. Such, indeed, is the mind of man!

ACT by means of non-action. Accomplish by not undertaking. Taste while a thing is tasteless. Consider small things as great and the few as though they were many. The most difficult tasks in the world should be performed while they are still easy. The greatest projects should be dealt with while they are still small. On this principle the sage never tackles things when they have become great, and so he achieves greatness. Many difficulties are encountered when men treat hard things as though they were easy. Therefore the sage, by treating easy things as though they were difficult, ends by finding nothing difficult.

EVERYONE in the world says that my Way is

great but seems to be impracticable. It is just because it is great that it seems impracticable. If it were practicable it would long ago have become insignificant. I have three treasures which I hold fast and preserve. The first is compassion. The second is frugality. The third is not daring to take pre-eminence in the world. Having compassion, I can be brave. Being frugal, I can be liberal. Because I do not seek pre-eminence in the world, I can become chief among those who serve. In these days the brave reject compassion, the liberal reject frugality, and those who are to the fore reject being behind. Such a way leads to death.

LXXX

WHEN I reach the extreme of emptiness and carefully guard my quietude, as myriad things interact with each other I contemplate their reversion (to non-being). Everything flourishes and then returns to its roots. This returning to the root is called quietude. Quietude is called reversion to one's destiny. Reversion to one's destiny is called a constant rule (of Nature). He who knows Nature's laws is enlightened. He who does not know the constant law (of Nature) acts foolishly and brings calamity. He who knows the constant law can be liberal-minded. Being liberal-minded, he is equitable. Being equitable, he is productive. Being productive, he is great. Being great, he is one with Tao. Being at one with Tao, he is long-lasting. To the end of his life he avoids danger.

REST only in inaction and all things will transform themselves. Relax your body, expel your intelligence, forget your natural relationships, and you will be in complete harmony with boundless cosmic forces. Release both mind and spirit, negate the soul, and all things will return to their root. When each one has returned to its root and is without perception, to the end of its days it will not be separated from that state which is turbid and undifferentiated. For when you perceive a thing you become separated from it. Do not inquire into its name. Do not probe into its nature. For all things live unto themselves.

★ LXXXII ★

WHICH lies closest, fame or self? Which counts for most, self or goods? Which is worse, gaining or losing? Therefore, the more things are cherished and the greater the trouble. The more things are hoarded the heavier the loss. He who is contented will not suffer humiliation. He who stays put will not be in danger. He will be able to remain for a long time.

★ LXXXIII ★

TO BE without tranquillity and contentment is to lack virtue. Without virtue no man on earth can survive for long.

★ LXXXIV ★

NOT to be entangled in worldly affairs, not to

make a show of material things, not be forward with individuals nor aggressive in a crowd, desiring peace for all the world so as to preserve the life of the people and nourish others as oneself, and when this is accomplished to be content, so manifesting purity of heart – the art of following Tao in ancient times lay in these things.

★ LXXXV ★

THE tortoise-shell has no 'self' and yet it has knowledge of great matters (it was used in divination). A lodestone has no 'self', and yet it has great strength. Bells and drums have no 'self' and yet they produce great sounds. Boats and carts have no 'self' and yet they can travel far. So it is that this body of mine, though it has knowledge, strength, sound and movement, does not necessarily have a 'self'.

★ LXXXVI ★

THE MAN who has forgotten self may be said to have entered heaven.

★ LXXXVII ★

WHEN the ancients talked about achieving their ambition they were not talking of carriages and ceremonial caps. They were simply talking of a joy to which nothing could be added. Nowadays, those who talk about achieving their ambition mean by it to have carriages and ceremonial caps. But carriages and ceremonial caps appertain to the body and not to life. When things arrive unexpectedly they should be accepted. Receive them, for you cannot prevent their arrival nor stop their departure. Therefore do not become recklessly ambitious over carriages and ceremonial caps. And if you find yourself in poverty and straitened circumstances you should not flatter the vulgar. In both these states one should maintain the same joy, and indeed, remain without a care. Nowadays, when something that one obtains is lost it brings unhappiness. From this we see that the joy which men possess soon deserts them. Therefore it is said, those who destroy themselves through material things and lose their inborn nature by vulgarity may be called topsy-turvy people.

★ LXXXVIII ★

THE MAN who considers wealth important finds himself unable to give up his salary. The man who considers his dignity important finds that he cannot relinquish his fame. The man who loves power cannot give up his authority over others. In holding on to these things men grow fearful, and they are grieved when they have to be relinquished. They never once pause for reflection so as to look into the reason for their ill-fortune. So heaven destroys them. Resentment and kindness, giving and receiving, reproval and instruction, life and death – these eight are the instruments of correction. Only one who complies with the great transformation and is without stain will be able to make use of them. Hence the saying: the corrector must be correct. The gates of heaven will not open to the mind that does not accept that this is so.

★ LXXXIX ★

HE who would assist a ruler in accordance with Tao will not use military force to seize the empire. For such methods are apt to recoil on oneself. In the places where armies are stationed, briars and thorns spring up. Famine inevitably follows in the wake of a great army. Therefore, a skilful general stops when he has attained his objective, he does not boast, nor make a show, nor indulge in pride. He achieves his objective because there is no alternative, and resorts to no more violence.

★ XC ★

WHEN the empire possesses Tao, horses which are used for travel are put to fertilizing the land. When the empire is without Tao, war horses are bred in the suburbs. There is no greater sin than covetousness. There is no greater disaster than not to know when one has enough. There is no fault more grievous than cupidity. For to know that enough is enough is true sufficiency.

★ XCI ★

I HAVE seen the failure of those who desired to seize the empire, so as to make it their own. The empire is a sacred vessel which cannot be appropriated. To appropriate it is to ruin it. To grasp it is to lose it. So it is with regard to things. Some go forward, some lag behind; some breathe in one way and some in another; some grow stronger and some grow weaker; some expand while others decline. This is why the sage rejects excess, extravagance and extremes.

★ XCII ★

IN an age of perfect government the worthy are not honoured and the talented are not employed. The ruler is like the highest branch on a tree, and the people are like forest deer. Living uprightly without knowing that such is righteousness, mutually loving without knowing that such is benevolence, sincere without knowing that such is loyalty, doing what is fitting without knowing that such is trustworthiness; the people wriggle about like worms helping one another. And on this account their behaviour leaves behind no trace, and their activities are not passed on.

★ XCIII ★

HEAVEN'S net is wide. Though its meshes are coarse nothing escapes.

★ XCIV ★

GREAT understanding is spacious. Small understanding is cramped. Great words are comprehensive. Small words are restrictive. In sleep the spirits of men are actively engaged. On wakening the body becomes busy, getting involved with all it meets. Daily the mind is engaged in contention, extending itself, striving, secreting, scared by little fears and overwhelmed by great fears. It flies off like an arrow from a cross-bow, adjudicating on matters of right and wrong. It holds to its own opinions as if it were on oath, and maintains that it is victorious. Then it goes into a decline, like autumn and winter, diminishing day by day. It becomes submerged in its activities so that it becomes impossible to make it turn back. It becomes obstinate, as if it were sealed up like an old drain. As the mind approaches death nothing can restore its active principle (yang).

★XCV★

NO ONE can see his reflection in running water, but only in still water. Only that which is itself still can bring stillness to all who seek after still-ness.

★XCVI★

BEASTS that feed on grass are not angry when their place of pasture is changed. Creatures that live in water do not grow angry at a change of water. They accept small changes so long as they do not lose what really matters. Joy, anger, sorrow, happiness do not enter the mind. Now as regards this world there is a unity pervading all things. Attain to this unity and become harmonized with it, and then your four limbs and the whole body will become as dust and filth, and life and death, beginning and end, will become as day and night and nothing will be able to confound you; far less such trifling things as gain and loss, misfortune and happiness.

★ XCVII ★

DO NOT the mountain forests and the wide-open plains bring us great joy and give us pleasure? Yet when pleasure ends grief follows. We cannot hinder the arrival of grief or pleasure and their departure we cannot hinder. Sad indeed! The generations of men are but 'things', in transit for awhile. They have knowledge only of what they happen to meet with, and no understanding of the things they do not encounter. Truly, what man cannot avoid is the lack of understanding of his own incapacity. Is it not a pity that men devote their attention to trying to avoid what cannot be avoided? Perfect speech is wordless. Perfect action is actionless. How shallow, indeed, only to know what all men equally know!

★ XCVIII ★

LIFE and death are a matter of destiny. They are as natural as the succession of night and day. The natural disposition of creatures is something that man can do nothing about. If a man is willing to regard heaven as his father so that he loves it, how much more should he love that which is eminently greater? If a man is willing to regard his ruler as superior to himself so that he will die for him, how much more should he be willing to die for truth?

65

LIFE and death, preservation and ruin, success and failure, poverty and riches, honour and disgrace, blame and praise, hunger, thirst, cold and heat – these are changes which take place in the order of things and are the workings of fate. Like day and night they alternate before us, and we know that we are unable to determine their origin. Consequently they are not worth causing a disturbance to our peace. They cannot enter into the sanctum of the spirit. Let harmony and delight prevail, and do not lose your contentment. Unceasingly, through day and night, let there be a springtime with all things. In this way you welcome and make a present-time within your own mind. This is called being talented in full measure.

WANG-NI said: As I see it, the rules of goodness and justice, and the paths of right and wrong are inextricably jumbled and confused. How can I possibly discriminate between them? Yeh-chüeh asked: If you do not know what is beneficial or harmful, then surely a 'perfected man' does not know either? Wang-ni replied: a perfect man is spiritual. He does not feel the heat when great swamps blaze, nor the cold when rivers freeze; when thunderbolts split open the mountains and violent gales sweep the seas, they cannot frighten him. Such a man rides upon the cloudy vapours, mounts up to the sun and moon, and wanders beyond the four seas. He is unaffected by life or death. How much less is he concerned with profit and loss?

★ CI ★

JOY and anger, grief and happiness, depression, changeability, inflexibility, modesty, wilfulness, candour and insolence – all these are but music from empty reeds, mushrooms sprouting from the dampness. Day and night succeed each other before us, and no one knows from whence they arise. So be it! So be it! Morning and evening make up the present, and it is that which constitutes living. Without them there would be no 'self', and without self there would be nothing for them to take hold of. This gets close to the matter, but I do not know what causes it all to be. There must be some controlling power, but I have certainly seen no trace of it. I believe it can act, but I do not see its form. It has factuality but is without form. My numerous joints, nine orifices and six organs constitute my body. Which should I hold most dear? Do we regard them as all equal, or is there a favourite? Are they not all servants? If they are all servants can they mutually keep themselves in order, or do they take turns at being master or servant? Surely there exists a true Master. That I should or should not seek to grasp his identity neither adds to nor subtracts from the truth of his existence.

★ CII ★

THE noble-minded man is ashamed when his words are in excess of his deeds.

67

★ CIII ★

THERE is no greater joy than to have no cause for sorrow; no greater riches than to know contentment with what one has; and to know that one does not know.

★ CIV ★

THERE are many people in the world who practise magical arts. Each one believes that his method cannot be improved upon. Where are the results of those arts which were practised by the men of olden times? I say that they are everywhere. The questions might be asked: From whence does the spiritual descend? From whence does enlightenment emerge? The sage gives birth to the one and the ruler brings the other to completion, but both have their origin in the One. A person who does not depart from his ancestors is called a natural man, but a person who does not depart from his spiritual essence is called a spiritual man. A person who does not depart from the true is called a perfected man. He who regards Nature as his ancestor, virtue as his root, and Tao as his gate remains as a sign through all change and transformation. Him we call a sage.

★ CV ★

TRUSTWORTHY speech is not fine-sounding. Fine-sounding speech is not trustworthy. Good ~eech is not disputatious for disputation is not good. The sage does not hoard. Having considered how to serve others, he still remains in surplus. Having considered how to give to others, he has more than enough left for himself. The Way of Heaven is to benefit and not to harm. The way of the sage is to act without striving.

★CVI★

THERE is a limit to life but there is no limit to knowledge. Danger occurs when the limited pursues after the unlimited. To know this and yet to pursue after knowledge is even more dangerous. Those who do good should avoid fame. Those who do evil need to avoid punishment. Make it your rule to follow a middle course, and you will be able to preserve your body, find fulfilment in life, support your parents, and live out your allotted term.

★CVII★

ONCE UPON A TIME Chuang-tzŭ dreamed that he was a butterfly, gaily flitting about, happily content to follow its fancy, and unaware that it was Chuang-tzŭ. Suddenly he awoke and was startled to find that he was Chuang-tzŭ. Now he knew not whether he was Chuang-tzŭ dreaming that he was a butterfly, or a butterfly dreaming that he was Chuang-tzŭ. Between Chuang-tzŭ and a butterfly there must indeed be some distinction. This may be called an experience of 'transformation'.

CHUANG-TZŬ said: How do I know that I am not deluded in my love of life? How do I know that, in hating death, I am not like one who left his home in youth and does not know the way back? Lady Li was the daughter of the frontier guard of Ai. When first she was taken captive by the Lord of Ch'in she wetted the lapel of her gown with her tears. But when she had settled in at the ruler's residence, sharing his couch and eating delicacies at his table, she repented of her tears. How do I know that the dead do not regret their former lust for life?

HE who dreams of drinking wine may weep when morning comes. He who dreams of weeping may be off to the hunt in the morning. During his dream he does not know that he is dreaming. It is only when he is wakened up that he knows that it was a dream. Someday there will be a great awakening. Then we shall know that this life is a great dream. Yet the foolish consider themselves to be awake, venturing to think that they understand things, calling one man ruler and another man herdsman – how stupid!

n archery contest, when the stakes are
are tiles a contestant shoots with skill.

When the stakes are belt buckles he becomes hesitant, and if the stakes are pure gold he becomes nervous and confused. There is no difference as to his skill but, because there is something he prizes, he allows outward considerations to weigh on his mind. All those who consider external things important are stupid within.

★CXI★

WHEN the shoe fits, the feet are forgotten. When a belt fits, the waist is forgotten. When the mind is suited, the understanding forgets matters of right and wrong. When there is no alteration within, and no following of what is without, one's affairs are suitably organized. Begin with what is suitable, and never do anything unsuitable, and one may forget the suitability of the suitable.

★CXII★

SUPPOSE a man is travelling in a boat across a river and an empty boat happens to bump into his boat. Though he may be a hot-tempered man he will not get angry. But if there is a man in the other boat he will call to him to pull away. If the call is unheeded he will call again. If still unheeded, he will call a third time but this time with a torrent of abuse. In the first case he was not angry, but now he is angry. In the first case there was an empty boat, but in this case there is someone there. If a man is able to empty himself

71

as he travels about the world, who can do him harm?

NAN-KUO-TZŬ-CHI sat leaning on a small table, gazing up at the sky and sighing. He seemed to be sick at heart as though he had lost a companion. Yen–ch'eṅg–tzŭ–yu was standing in attendance before him and said: What is this? Can you cause your body to become like dried-up wood and your mind like dead ashes? The person who is now leaning on the table is not like the one who was leaning on it before. Tzŭ-chi replied: A good question! Just now I lost myself. Do you understand? You hear the music of men but not the music of earth. You hear the music of earth but not the music of heaven. Tzŭ-yu replied: May I ask the meaning of this? Tzŭ-chi said: The breathing forth of the great clod [Tao] is called the 'wind'. Sometimes it is inactive, but when it is active angry howling arises from ten thousand openings. Have you not heard the roaring of the wind? There is the fearsome swaying of the trees in the mountain forests; the openings and hollow spaces in great trees of a hundred spans' girth, like noses, mouths and ears, like gouges, bowls and mortars, like rifts and runnels; they roar and whistle, blow out and in, shout and moan, wail and howl, starting from a hiss and ending with a roar. ⸮en the zephyrs blow their chorus sounds faint, ⸮en the fierce gales arise they are mighty. ⸮erce gale is overpast all the hollows become vacant, and then surely it is as though all the shaking and trembling had not been seen. Tzǔ-yu said: The music of earth, then, is the sound from all these hollows, just as man's music is made from a hollow reed. But may I ask: What is the music of heaven? Tzǔ-chi replied: It is blowing in a multitude of ways, allowing each thing to be itself and to produce its own sound. The question is: What is it that stimulates them?

★ CXIV ★

CONFUSED, boundless and formless, restlessly changing: are we dead; are we alive; are we in union with heaven and earth? Do our spirit and intelligence go away somewhere? Are we troubled as to what our end might be? Or are we indifferent as to where we are going? Creation wraps us round but provides no adequate resting-place. In ancient times, those who followed the art of Tao asked questions like these. Chuang-tzǔ also heard their views and delighted in them.

★ CXV ★

A COOK called Ting was cutting up an ox for Lord Hui of Wên. Every slick of the hand, every heave of the shoulder, every stance of the foot, every thrust of the knee – all in perfect rhythm as, with the sound of tearing flesh the knife sliced forward. It was like the 'dance of the mulberry grove' or like the harmonies of *ching-shou* music.

Lord Hui of Wên said Ah me! What excellence! Can it be that skill can reach such perfection? Cook Ting put down his knife and replied: That which I prize is Tao, and Tao goes beyond skill. When first I began to cut up an ox I saw only the ox itself. After three years I no longer saw the ox as a whole, and now it is through the spirit that I make my approach and not through the physical sight. Senses and understanding cease and the spirit takes over the action. I rely on the principles of nature, strike where there are great spaces, follow through the hidden openings, accept things as they are, never touching the ligaments and tendons, much less the main joints. A good cook changes his knife once a year because he cuts. An ordinary cook changes his knife once a month because he hacks. This knife of mine has lasted nineteen years and has cut up several thousand oxen, and yet the blade is as if it had just left the whetstone. There is space between the joints, and the knife-edge has no thickness. If what is without thickness enters where there is space there is plenty of room, and more than enough in which to manipulate the blade. That is why, after nineteen years, my knife is as keen as if it had just left the whetstone. Nevertheless, each time that I meet with any complications I take precautions. I look carefully, act slowly, and with the slightest movement of the knife the flesh falls apart like a clod of earth crumbling to the ground. Holding my knife I stand there, looking around exceedingly gratified. Then I clean my knife and put it away. How excellent, said the Lord of Wên, by listening to the words of cook Ting I have learned the way to take care of my life.

★CXVI★

ON the death of Lao-tzŭ, Chin-shih said: Your Master came at the time appointed, and at the appointed time he has departed. If one is in accord with one's time and place, grief and pleasure cannot enter in. In olden times this was called 'freedom from bondage'. When a faggot is burned out the fire passes on, and no one knows its final end.

★CXVII★

WHEN a carpenter called Shih was on his way to the state of Ch'i he arrived at a place called Ch'u-yüan where he saw the [sacred] oak tree of the village shrine. It was so huge that it could give shade to several thousand oxen. In girth it was a hundred span, and it seemed to tower over the nearby hills, its lowest branches spreading out eighty feet from the ground. More than ten of these branches could have been fashioned into boats. The place was like a market for the number of sightseers, but the carpenter took no notice, and went on his way without stopping. His apprentice stared his fill and then ran after carpenter Shih and said: From the time I took up my axe and became your apprentice I have never seen such excellent timber. But you cannot even stop to look at it. You just go right on. Why is this? Carpenter Shih replied: Enough! Don't say any

75

more. As wood the tree is useless. Make boats of it and they would sink. Make coffins and they would rot. Make utensils and they would break. Try to use it to make doors and windows and they would exude resin like pine. Think of using it for pillars and they would become worm-eaten. This is a useless tree, and there is nothing for which it can be used. It is because of this that it has reached such a great age. The apprentice said: If it is so keen on being useless, why does it serve a shrine? Hush, said carpenter Shih, Not a word! It is simply standing there so that those who have no understanding will not abuse it. If it were not at the shrine, would it not be in danger of being cut down? Furthermore, its method of protecting itself is not like that of the multitude. You are a long way out if you judge it by ordinary standards.

* CXVIII *

NAN-P'O-TZǓ-K'UEI asked a hunchback woman: How is it that, although you are old in years, your complexion is like that of a child? She replied: Have you heard tell of Tao? Tzǔ-k'uei asked: Can Tao be learnt? No, surely, she replied, that could not possibly be. In any case, you are not the man to do it. Now consider P'u-liang-i. He has the talents of a sage but not the Tao of a sage, whereas I possess the Tao of a sage but am without the talents. I had a desire to teach him, for it seemed to me that he might attain to sagehood. But it was not possible, though it seemed easy that one who had the Tao of a sage should be able to teach one who has the talents of a sage. So I stayed and taught him for three days, after which he was able to detach his mind from the world. Having achieved that, I kept at it for another seven days, and then he could detach his mind from material things. After another nine days he could detach himself from life. Once he had detached himself from life he was able to reach the dawn of perception, and with dawning perception he could see the One. Seeing the One, he could eliminate past and present. There being no past or present, he was able to enter where there is neither death nor life. That [Tao] which destroys life does not itself die, and that which gives birth to life does not itself live. Considered as 'something', there is nothing that it does not send off and nothing that it does not welcome; nothing that it does not destroy and nothing that it does not bring to completion. Its name is 'tranquillity in struggle', for after struggle it attains completion.

★ CXIX ★

FOUR MEN, Tzŭ-ssu, Tzŭ-yu, Tzŭ-li and Tzŭ-lai, were discussing things together. The remark was made: Whoever is able to consider non-being as the head, life as the spine, and death as the rump, whoever knows the essential unity between life and death, existence and non-existence, that man shall be our friend. The four men looked at each other and smiled. Their minds being all of one accord, they became fast friends. Suddenly

Tzǔ-yu fell ill and Tzǔ-ssu went to enquire as to how he was. Extraordinary! said Tzǔ-yu, that the creator should make me crooked like this. My spine is curved like a hunchback, my vital organs are in disarray, my chin hidden in my navel and my shoulders higher than my head, with my queue pointing to the sky. The forces of yin and yang are all in confusion. Yet his mind was untroubled and at peace. He limped over to a well and looking at his reflection he sighed: Ah me! That the creator should make me all crooked like this! Tzǔ-ssu asked : Are you not resentful? No, he replied, why should I be resentful? Suppose that in process of transformation my left arm becomes a rooster. Then with it I will herald the dawn. And if my right arm becomes a crossbow, I will shoot down a bird to broil. And if my buttocks are turned into wheels, with my spirit for a horse I will mount up and ride off, with no more need for a carriage. Accepting as timely both birth and death, content with both time and place, neither joy nor sorrow can enter in. The men of old called it 'freedom from suspense'. Those who cannot free themselves are bound by material things. Yet material things can never be superior to Heaven. How then could I be resentful?

★CXX★

THE RULER of the Southern Sea was called 'hasty' (Shu). The ruler of the Northern Sea was called 'careless' (Hu), and the ruler of the Central Region was called 'chaos' (Hun-tun). From time to time Shu and Hu would meet together in the territory of Hun-tun, who would entertain them extremely well. So Shu and Hu deliberated how best they could requite Hun-tun for his kindness. They said: All creatures have seven orifices for seeing, eating, hearing and breathing. Hun-tun alone is without them. Let us try to bore some for him. So each day they bored an opening. On the seventh day Hun-tun died!

★CXXI★

FOR nineteen years Huang-ti reigned as Son of Heaven, and his commands prevailed throughout the world. Having heard that Master Kuang-ch'êng resided in the realm of vacuous totality above the Pole Star, he went off to interview him, and said: I have heard, master, that you have attained to the most perfect Tao. I venture to ask you concerning the essence of perfect Tao. I desire to apprehend the essence of heaven and earth, for by that means I can aid the five grains to grow and so nourish the common people. I would also like to control the forces of yin and yang so as to bring harmony to all living things. Kuang-ch'êng replied: The matter you desire to inquire into concerns the nature of things, but what you desire to control concerns the dissolution of things. From the time that you have ruled over the world it has rained before the misty vapours have had time to collect. Vegetation has withered before it has had time to mature. The light of sun and moon have become increasingly deficient. You

79

are a great talker and have the mind of a flatterer. What is the good of talking with you about perfect Tao? Huang-ti withdrew, renounced his throne, built a solitary dwelling, and with white rushes for a mat lived for three months in retirement. Then once again he went for an interview. Master Kuang-ch'êng was reclining in a position facing south (that of a superior). Huang-ti assumed a humble posture, approached on his knees, kowtowed twice, and petitioning humbly said: I have heard that my master is proficient in the most perfect Tao. I dare to ask how one can master one's body so as to attain to longevity. Master Kuang-ch'êng hastily arose and said: An excellent question indeed! Come, and I will speak with you of perfect Tao. In essence it is deep and profound. At the limit of perfect Tao there is mystery and silence. Shutting out sight and sound, with your body in a correct posture, enfold your spirit in tranquillity. You must become still. You must become pure. Avoid wearying your body or agitating your mind. Then you can live a long life. When there is nothing for the eye to see, nothing for the ear to hear, nothing for the mind to know, your spirit takes care of your body and your body lives long. Take care of what lies within. Shut yourself off from what lies without. Much knowledge will do harm. I will cause you to follow through to the heights of great illumination, to the very source of yang. I will cause you to enter the gates of darkness and mystery, the very source of yin. Heaven and earth have their governors. Yin and yang have their storehouses. Carefully guard yourself, and this thing [Tao] will of itself grow strong. I myself guard its unity so as to rest in its harmony. Consequently, for twelve hundred years I have been cultivating myself and my body has not decayed. Huang-ti humbly bowed his head twice and said: Master Kuang, you should indeed be called a heavenly being. Kuang-ch'êng replied: Come, I will instruct you. This thing [Tao] is inexhaustible, yet all men consider that it has an end. It is unfathomable, yet all men consider that it has a limit. He who obtains this Tao of mine will see the light above and be as dust below. Now all these created things are born of dust, and to the dust they will return. Now I am going to leave you so that I may enter the gates of the infinite, that I may wander in limitless fields. I shall mingle as one with the light of the sun and moon. I shall partake of the constancy of heaven and earth. How confused is anyone who thinks he is able to resist me. How stupid is he who is removed far from me. Men become exhausted and they die. I alone survive.

★ CXXII ★

TZŬ-KUNG journeyed to the state of Ch'u, and on his way bank to the state of Chin, as he passed along the south bank of the river Han he saw an old man preparing his vegetable plot. He emerged from a sunken path to a well and was carrying a pitcher to do his watering. He was making strenuous efforts and using much energy, only to produce a meagre result. Tzŭ-kung said to him: There is a machine for this kind of work. In one day you could water a hundred plots with very little effort and with great results. Wouldn't you like one? The gardener raised his head, looked at him and said: How does it work? Tzŭ-kung replied: It is a machine shaped out of wood, heavy behind and light in front. It raises up the water so that it flows out in great abundance. It is called a well-sweep. The gardener flushed angrily and then laughed saying: I have heard my teacher say that the production of machinery is evidence of cunning dealings. Cunning dealings are evidence of cunning minds. When there is a cunning mind within one's purity and simplicity are impaired. When purity and simplicity are impaired the life of the spirit is unsettled, and when the life of the spirit is unsettled there is no place for Tao to reside. It is not that I do not know about the machine. I should be ashamed to use it.

* CXXIII *

THE SEA-GOD Jo of the Northern Sea said: A frog in a well, restricted in his environment, is unable to talk about the ocean. A summer insect, confined to its season, cannot talk about ice. A poor village scholar, restricted by his doctrines, cannot discuss Tao. Now when someone leaves his own cliffs and river banks to gaze upon the mighty ocean, he is able to perceive his own pettiness and can then begin to discuss the Great Principle.

MASTER LIEH-TZǓ was questioning the frontier guard Yin. He said: The perfect man can walk under water without suffocating; can tread on fire without being burnt; can travel high above creation without being frightened. I would like to ask how he is able to do these things. The frontier guard Yin replied: This is because he guards his own vital spirit. It is not due to attainments such as knowledge, skill, determination or daring. Stay awhile and I will explain. All things that have faces, voices, forms, colours, are 'things'. How is it possible for things to be mutually distant from each other? How can it be sufficient to think of one thing preceding another? They are all simply forms and colours. Now that which creates 'things' is formless, and that which brings them to an end is changeless. Whoever is able to obtain this and probe into it thoroughly, how can any thing stop him? Such a one will settle into his place in life, hiding away in periods of change, roaming where all things have their beginning and end, unifying his nature, nourishing his vital breath, cherishing his virtue; and in that way he is in rapport with that which creates all being. One who acts in this way guards and perfects his heaven-born nature. His spirit is faultless. How then can any external thing trouble him?

A WOODCARVER called Ch'ing was carving

wood to make a bell-frame. When it was finished all who saw it marvelled, for it seemed to be the work of spirits. When the Marquis of Lu saw it he asked: What kind of art is this of yours to make such a thing? He replied: I am a simple workman. How can I possess any art? But there is one thing. When I am about to make a bell-frame I never allow myself to waste my vital energy. I fast so as to calm my mind. When I have fasted for three days I think no more about congratulations, rewards, titles or emoluments. When I have fasted for five days I no longer think of praise or blame, skill or clumsiness. When I have fasted for seven days I suddenly forget about my four limbs and my bodily form. When that time arrives I am no longer conscious of the ruler's court. There remains only my skill and the surroundings fade away. Thereupon I enter a mountain forest and examine the nature of the trees. Having found one of suitable form I see the bell-frame there in perfection, and then I set my hand to the task. If the wood is unsuitable I discard it. In that way I match nature with nature. This, no doubt, is the reason why the finished work is deemed to be the work of spirits.

* CXXVI *

LONG AGO there was a bird which alighted in the suburb of the capital of the state of Lu. The ruler was delighted with it. He had the 'Tai-lao' sacrifices prepared for it to feed on, and the emperor Shun's music played for its enjoyment. But the bird began to look miserable and dazed. It did not venture to eat or drink. This is what may be called 'nourishing a bird with the food that nourishes oneself'. Now if you want to nourish a bird it would be best to let it roost deep in the forest, or drift on the lakes and rivers feeding on loaches. In that way it would rest content.

★ CXXVII ★

THERE was a man who feared his own shadow and hated his footprints. He tried to rid himself of them by running away. But the more he lifted his feet and the more footprints he made, and however fast he ran his shadow never left him. Still thinking that he was running too slowly, he quickened his pace and ran on without stopping till his strength gave out and he dropped down dead. He did not understand that if he had stayed in the shade he would have lost his shadow, and by standing still he would have ceased making footprints. How very stupid!

★ CXXVIII ★

KUNG-SUN-LUNG (the Logician) said to Prince Mou of Wei: When I was young I studied the ways of various teachers, and when I grew up I had a clear understanding of benevolence and righteousness. I could also reconcile sameness with difference, and confuse people with notions of 'hard' and 'white'. I could prove that 'so' is 'not so', and that the possible is impossible. I

85

exhausted the wisdom of a hundred schools and probed into the arguments of a host of speakers. I thought of myself as being most accomplished. But now that I have heard the words of Chuang-tzǔ I am flustered by their strangeness. I cannot tell whether it is that my arguments are inadequate or whether my understanding is no match for his. I am afraid to open my mouth, and I ask you to give me your advice. Prince Mou leaned upon a table, heaved a great sigh and gazed up to heaven. Then with a smile he said: Have you ever heard of the frog in a dilapidated well. When in conversation with the turtle of the Eastern Sea he said: How happy I am! I leap out on to a beam over the shaft of the well, or I enter into a hole in the wall where a tile is missing, and there I take my rest. I dive into the water and it supports my armpits and my chin. I play around in the mud, let my feet and ankles sink in, and look round on the mosquito larvae, the crabs and tadpoles, and none of them can compare with me. The joy of exercising authority over the waters of the well and sitting astride it is the best thing there is. Dear Sir, why don't you come and enter in sometime, and see for yourself? Before the left foot of the turtle of the Eastern Sea could enter the well his right knee got wedged fast. So he shrank back and withdrew himself. Then he spoke to the frog about the ocean: A thousand miles are insufficient to measure its extent. A thousand fathoms will not plumb its depth. Never to increase or diminish not for an instant nor for eternity, never to advance or recede by much or by little; that is the great joy of the Eastern Sea. When the frog in the dilapidated well heard this he was crestfallen and quite put out of countenance. Now your comprehension knows not the limits of right and wrong. Your desire to probe into the meaning of Chuang-tzǔ's words is like employing a mosquito to carry a mountain, or like a millipede racing across the Yellow River. It is quite certain that you will not succeed in your task.

★ CXXIX ★

CHUANG-TZǓ was fishing in the river P'u. The king of Ch'u sent two officials to give him a message: I would like you to trouble yourself with the administration of my state. Chuang-tzǔ pointed with his fishing rod, and without looking their way he said: I have heard that Ch'u possesses a sacred tortoise which has been dead for three thousand years. The king had it wrapped up and placed in a casket, and he stores it high up in the ancestral temple. Now this tortoise, would it rather be dead with its bones preserved and honoured, or would it rather be alive with its tail dragging in the mud? The two officials replied that it would rather be alive with its tail dragging in the mud. Be off with you, said Chuang-tzǔ, I prefer to drag my tail in the mud!

★ CXXX ★

THE WIFE of Chuang-tzǔ died and his friend Hui-tzǔ went to condole with him. Chuang-tzǔ was sitting with his legs spread out, pounding on a tub and singing. Hui-tzǔ said: Here is someone who has lived with you, brought up your children, and grown old. Not to weep at her death is surely bad enough, but to beat on a tub and sing, surely that is going too far. Chuang-tzǔ replied: Not so. At first, when she died, how is it possible that I should not have felt grief? But I pondered over her beginning before she was born; not merely before she was born but when as yet there was no body; not merely was there no body but not even the vital spirit. Within an inchoate confusion there took place a transformation and there was vital spirit. The vital spirit was transformed and there came forth form, and with the transformation of form there was life. Now once again there is a transformation and she has died. What happened may be compared to the progression of the four seasons – spring, summer, autumn, winter. Now she is lying in peace in a large room. For me to follow after her weeping and wailing would be an indication that I have no thorough understanding of human destiny. So I stopped grieving.

★CXXXI★

CHUANG-TZǓ was about to die, and his disciples wanted to give him a sumptuous funeral. Chuang-tzǔ said: I would like to have heaven and earth for my inner and outer coffins; the sun and moon to be my jade disks; the host of stars to be my pearly ornaments; and all creation to be my 'sending off' gifts. Are not the furnishings of my funeral already prepared? How can anything be added to these? The disciples answered: We fear that the kites will feed on our Master. Then Chuang-tzŭ said: Above ground I should be eaten by kites, below ground by ants. Would it not be unfair to take from the one in order to give to the other?

★ CXXXII ★

FROM scrolls hung in a Taoist temple: No matter how deceitful you are, or how bad, or how much you act against your conscience, Heaven is always watching you. I am in control of this world and the next, and it is my courage which protects the city and its inhabitants. My power is used to punish and reward. My grace overspreads a multitude of men.

SOURCES OF THE QUOTATIONS

Chuang-tzǔ XI-XII, XVII-XIX, XXI-XXIII,
XXXIV-XXXVI, XXXVIII, XLI-XLII,
LI-LXI, LXIII, LXV, LXVIII-LXXI,
LXXVII, LXXXI, LXXXIII-LXXXIV,
LXXXVI-LXXXVIII, XCII, XCIV-CI,
CIV, CVI-CXXXI

Han-fei-tzǔ II

Ho-kuan-tzǔ XXVI

Huai-nan-tzǔ X, XXV, XXVII, XXX,
XXXII-XXXIII, LXVII

Kuan-tzǔ III, XXVIII

Kuan-yin-tzǔ IX, LXXXV

Kuei-ku-tzǔ V

Liu-pu-wei XX

Shu-chu-tzǔ LXXV

Tao-Tê-Ching I, IV, VI-VIII, XIII-XVI, XXIV,
XXIX, XXXVII, XXXIX-XL, XLIII-L,
LXIV, LXVI, LXXII-LXXIV, LXXVI,
LXXVIII-LXXX, LXXXII, LXXXIX-XCI,
XCIII, CV

Tung-ku-chang XXXI

Wang-ch'ung LXII

Attributed to Lao-tzǔ CII-CIII

Taoist scrolls CXXXII